I0617453

The Adoration

The original title, *La adoración*, was first published in 2012 by DVD Ediciones, Barcelona, Spain. © Juan Andrés García Román, 2012

© of this edition: Quantum Prose, 2023

Editorial Director: Marta del Pozo
Editorial Advisor: Gregg Harper

Cover Photography: *Ode to Sierpiński 4* © Katherine Crippen, 2019

ISBN: 979-8-9886901-0-8
Library of Congress Control Number: 2023941963

Quantum Prose is a 501 (c) (3) non-profit organization incorporated in New York City, NY

quantumprosebooks@gmail.com
www.quantumprose.org

With the support of

AC/E
ACCIÓN CULTURAL
ESPAÑOLA

The Adoration

Juan Andrés García Román

~

Translated by Nick Rattner

QUANTUM PROSE

CONTENTS

For Laura

THE BURNING BUSH IN SPRING

And I wished to become extinct with the great beasts, the great beasts that made up your soul when you cast your flashlight there. Escaped from the irony of time. The foolish, the clumsy, the innocent, the obsolete covered all at once in a dignity, as though feathered. Your gaze. Never studious, no smoke of forms, not some contortionist entering through the eye of a needle. No. You were your body and therein you loved, you were space. And if geraniums via velveteen put out peaches, or the rosebush fruited a heart, that was not, for you, mere function: things, how to put it, things flourished by submersing themselves in their own colors, in your feeling. Or because you simmered your creation with the heat from Moses's burning bush, according to the precise formula for childhood, they distilled to their essences, innocent, incessant inside their frames. In this way your kindness drove the Ganges down skyscraper staircases. And who cares if the centipede had ninety-nine feet; you would ride piggyback on the shoulders of your soul and call out his name, just as the heartbeat inside you discovered the world, the hollow where being would not be lonely.

THE ADORATION

If from loving we did not actually die,
then maybe it was not a great love,
or perhaps it was.

GIANNI VATTIMO

DRAMATIS PERSONÆ

EXPOSITO
The four-eyes I, a weirdo or even a harlequin

JUAN BOY
Sherpa

STERNLI
Astrologer of the Homeland, stepfather to Ancila and Juan Boy

THE ASTROLOGER'S WIFE
Sick mother of Ancila and Juan Boy

ANCILA
Mystic Seamstress of the Homeland

KIMBERLY CLARK,
Anthropologist, Leader

ARMITAGE SHANKS
Prophet, Leader

The Count SOBABYETTE
Noble with a candle hand

NUTCRACKER
The figurine, Sobabyette's lone soldier

Sobabyette's DOGS
Among them, KANGUNO

THE PHILOSOPHER
Impotent and autistic

CHAPTER 1. THE MOUNTAIN HAMLET

One day I knock on the astrologer's door. A boy opens it. In a room where dawn is breaking, a man and a woman. The woman is sick. Her husband fans her with a dead pigeon. He calls to the boy:

–Tend to your mother.

The man bounds from the bed. His face narrows through his beard.

–Your right hand –he orders.

And I obey, opening my palm so eagerly that the lines pop out.

–Exposito, terrible, just terrible!

–That's right, I want to die for beauty –I said. And I paused, for upon entering the room my glasses had blushed and fogged over. For the first time I recognized myself within my consciousness, far from you; words came apart and came back together and through their fissures trickled in the cold. She's not here and I am, you understand? –And while the man busied himself stashing the pigeon in a trunk, my anxiety dissipated: –invalidating history, life continues, to my dismay: Why does the sun choose the edges? May it extinguish in splendor, oh center of the vault that the butterfly points to with wings folded, a red blade perfectly perpendicular to the heavens!

–Monstruous, truly. In any event, you will need a Sherpa for your aesthetic journey. You know, altitude sickness… My boy…

A buzzing sound like radio interference crests, what turns out to be the woman's rasp:

–Nathanial, no! He's just a kid, ack, ack!

–A Sherpa? A Sherpa, you really think…?

–Of course!

The child approaches:

–I am Juan Boy. –And he holds out his little hand.

CHAPTER 2. A PALACE IS CONTAINED IN ITS CARRIAGES

The wind was blowing. I had opened the window, and it was blowing, the wind was blowing the curtain, its pattern of checkerboards having turned into rhombuses. The Sherpa, who must have awoken earlier:

–I'm cold. I need a coat.

–Let's go.

And go we did. Knock-knock. The door to the seamstress' shop opens, a dim light flickering within. A girl:

–My name is Ancila.

–I am Exposito. –My glasses fogged over again, but cockiness, no, I didn't want for cockiness: – When you scale Face A of K2 it won't be the same as when you descend, neither can rocks nor streams be the same. A mountain exists only when you climb it and when you climb down, it vanishes. How does one climb a mountain forever, in time and in space?

–Juan is no Sherpa, he's just a boy. My mother let you bring him? Did my stepfather sell him to you? If you hand over the child, I'll help you. You want to reach a castle, but you're not sure if it exists; therefore, venture neither faster nor higher, but change carriages.

–What are you saying? Whether a count arrives to one palace or another depends entirely on the shape of his carriage?

–Exposito, each day He moves one centimeter further from our cuddly mimesis. Meanwhile, men pursue Him with bevels and ladders. Many will ask where birds sleep on an island without trees. Some, spiritualists in loose fitting garbs, will respond that they are among the stars, but the wisest will tell you that they sleep on the ground. That the birds themselves configure the island. Its most intimate flight. Does that then mean we know nothing of Him? Nothing, Exposito?

–Well, I don't really know and…–I was wondering why everyone in the Homeland speaks of "Him" and of the heavens. What could possibly be so special about a grave-digger and his hateful winepress? Personally, I have no wish for comfort and if I desired for our story to reach its conclusion, I would think not of death, but of more life.

Yet Ancila continued:

–Yes, we know, of course. No beyond exists, but limits, yes. Though they don't appear as such, there are footprints all the same, reflections, sargassum from another world the day after a storm. Rapturous animals, bees inside honey.

Birds, bees: an entire fauna trotted by in Ancila's arguments. Which is why I thought of the great beasts that were your soul when you cast your flashlight there. I climbed atop a stool and recited:

Whales are shadows of clouds,
and bring storms, too;
stirred up thunderclaps
they squawk with language.

In the meantime, Ancila had put her hands to work. She insisted that if her brother were to remain in my care we should be properly attired. She came up with a quick fix, one commensurate with our scant resources; she took my fur coat, clipped cloth from its back, and with this cloth fashioned two small arms, fitting one to each side of my chest. The boy was meant to fit inside these little arms and to pop his head out where I would leave a button unfastened.

And so it was, the two of us just so in the same fur coat, reaching out our four arms, venturing into another day and another chapter. During all this, the wind brought forth another season, fluttering our garbs, filling the countryside with the confidences of the men of cloth.

CHAPTER 3. THE TWO CHAMELEONS
POSIBL AN' MENTE

The following day we set off from the Mountain Hamlet, following the course of a river, a river that actually was a bed of flowing blonde hair bordered by shepherds aching with love.

But I had no desire to hear their tired old palavers. No desire to hear about crystal, rose, or lily waters. Quite the opposite, I forced myself to think of platypuses, mangoes, and other hybrids, for I knew that an endemic plant or animal would tamp down associative thinking. To reach where you were, truly, to speak with you…this, in any case, words fail to achieve, no matter their order. Better to be shipwrecked in language, swim across the ocean, reach an island. Wasn't that also Ancila the Seamstress' advice? Perhaps. I wasn't so sure.

Some two hundred meters from there, or, rather, around two hundred leaps and bounds, we came upon an abandoned train station. Then the Sherpa slipped out of his get-up and placed an ear on the track:

–What do you hear? Is it on its way? Is it her? Do you hear her voice?

–I hear a planet of nettles, he replied.

Though this seemed a bad omen, it awoke my curiosity and, like him, I brought my ear close, though I heard nothing, much less anything as substantial as a planet.

–Tell me, why did you say a planet of nettles? A planet all covered in nettles? Is something bad going to happen? Have you heard the seven trumpets, glaciers tumbling into black holes?

He offered no reply for the timid boy had gone on ahead and with hands on hips stood staring at his giant's shadow in a wheat field. Up ahead loomed Thy Neighbor Forest, cliffs veiled by Thy Neighbor Clouds, and the blonde river tumbling through a narrow pass. Out of nowhere a curling wind picked up. A flock of white birds passed, their shadows depositing upon the outcrops in the landscape a thin blanket of snow.

–That is the way, he said.

A red forest parted before our feet, delivering us to a mountain shaped like a suitcase. In accordance with their cycle, the oldest of the trees launched themselves upwards on the poles of their trunks until they turned into clouds and rained down. But the Sherpa was spooked:

–You don't hear the doors slamming?

–Easy boy, it's only the wind.

–Why can't you hear them? All the doors are open!

Because, he explained to me, the distance that lies between two tree trunks in a forest is always a door. And each forest trunk forms a door with all the other trunks, not only with those next to it, but with those far off ones, too. In contrast to him, I was clearly either a rather analytical or a rather mature person as I heard, at most, one door slam. How I envied the Sherpa! In his eyes, the forest existed in a state of feverish consciousness: narrow, inconceivable doors, doors all tall and twisted. Doubtless, the lack inside his perspective populated his world with elves.

By then night had fallen. The sky was covered by Thy Neighbor Clouds, and we stopped when we encountered an abandoned hut.

I spent the whole afternoon going in circles about the origin of the world before falling fast asleep. I dreamed of two albino chameleons, each one a habitat for the other; they floated along in space until figuring out their first color. Later, between them, other colors would appear: one the green of your shirt, the other of your grey shirt. Later you arrived and I shouted:

> ≈ Run to the door that's shaped like you. The door that your body will activate like a key and which will bring you to my side, identical for all time. Oh death, oh chameleon completely mine!

That's what I was up to when the Sherpa, unable to sleep on account of the slamming doors, came over to me and blew out my fitful sleep with a breath.

–What happens now? I asked him.

I could barely see but could make out beside me a pair of open clippers. He had been cutting his fingernails and toenails. Then he held his palm open – where the lines of love and of life ran close as the Tigris and Euphrates – and into my hands deposited his clippings, adding:

–In case one day you can't see the moon.

I didn't understand, for back then I couldn't imagine a day I'd be imprisoned and would have to fashion a lunar calendar with those nails and the buttons from my fur coat. So I simply deposited his nails in my left pocket, took his hand and inserted it into my right, the pocket full of laces, those girlhood laces of yours I rubbed to soothe myself.

A few minutes later, the two of us were snoring.

CHAPTER 4. WITH EARTHQUAKES GOD ROCKS THE CRADLE OF THE ORPHANS

My dream deeply buried in morning.

Until a door slides open and in strolls a beetle rolling a snow-ball. Really? And I peered out the window: not one tree named I, all trees named you, ils s'appellent elles, or, in other words, it snowed!

The Sherpa leaps into my fur coat and, four-armed, we play at juggling snowballs. Until the snow gets glum, gets glum.

For you yourself were childhood, the so small room.

Yes, childhood, but why? What did it have to do with you? I thought: to be, with no time passing. As holding light childhood grows, in its own effigy, a process that, if we think about it, never stops, only fades. Or we fade. Wander off. Living, yes, okay. And it could even be said that, from behind ever-changing foliage, we may catch sight of childhood's palace, the one faith was lost in, still awaiting us.

Bored, the Sherpa chased after a squirrel while I paced these stirred up semantic fields:

> If this voice calls you but can't
> bring you near
> why should I have it at all?

So I can write come here
and if you do, okay,
and if you don't, oh no?
Song of mine grow not weary
not from the lady who turned
her back to us
nor from yesterday's rose
scale instead the lightning's strike
and so sensing and speaking
at once, being and wasing,
rise, go, be.

And then, with a clenched fist:

–Oh, this freedom of mine shall put an end to the stubborn eternity of beauty!

Upon the forest's winter bone, mist with its folds swaddled a sun, veiled and transvestite, like a moon but fuller. And so a drunk and sleepy scene continued until two men came through one of the forest doors.

–Save me from this disastrous course! –I found the nerve to shout to them–, Don't become butterflies of August nights: neither lantern nor moon, becoming one and the same, ships heading into their own forms, their St. Elmo's fires…

–I am here for you! –said one of them, apparently an anthropologist.

–I am forlorn, came the other, who turned out to be a

prophet.

The first one approached clutchingly and said:

> –My name is Kimberly Clark and I name you Chancellor of our Intelligentsia.

The second approached covetously and seconded:

> –My name is Armitage Shanks. Exposito, we require your symbols. They are sign posts for the abandoned nest of the Spirit.

Not knowing how to respond, clapping them on their shoulders, I resorted to stock phrases:

> –Noble Kimberly and beloved Armitage…

But as I had no clue how to continue, Kimberly Clark stepped in:

> –In any case, your love is a convention, a convent, my friend. Not even gender is given, recall that the sex of reptiles is determined by the temperature of eggs buried at a certain depth and…

Armitage Shanks interrupted him:

> –This is not the issue, Kimberly, reptiles slither, just like the dead. The main thing is man, who, tragically upright, picks fruit from trees, hangs himself, or sets the time of dad's carillon. We await you in our works: the rolling pin and horizon line!

But that day it was I who interrupted the two of them:

> –No, friends, the fish swims not because there is water, but because it is fish. We are neither terrestrial nor celestial circumstances; read it in our hands, we are free.

At that moment, all Armitage Shanks or Kimberly Clarke could do was stare at their hands. Then did they speak…

CHAPTER 5. CATHEDRALS

...and they continued speaking until spring.

Kimberly Clark, in this his first youthful fervor, taught me how critical it was to keep memory active, performing his exercises:

> –Imagine a humanity in which the son puts on his hat and on top of it all the ascendents he remembers, grandpatrala and grandpatralala. Men with towers of hats on their heads are called cathedrals, cathedral spires, or simply "fathers" or "masters." But this comes at the cost of colossal headaches. You must set time to the correct hour. Don't worry about our differences, the moment is now! Noble Exposito and beloved Armitage! Spring has come...look, look at the mute, his sign language is coming into bloom, an art akin to pantomime.

All the while Armitage Shanks kept right in stride:

–Can't you hear it drawing near...the Adoration?

CHAPTER 6. THE BUNKBEDS OF BABEL

And indeed, we hear branches clattering, and I see the Sherpa, his face a mask of fear, coming through the forest gates, and behind him a throng so heterogenous and frenzied that it spooked me. The Sherpa leaps inside my fur coat, and Shanks says:

> –I present to you the very best, our men, with who we will cross Thy Neighbor Mountains and Forests to the Spirit Vale. We will establish a vigilant society and your poetry, Exposito, will be the star that tethers the port, our lighthouse. The anointed shall join our ranks, that mighty race of orphans.

As the procession approaches, however, I consider the delirium of Armitage Shanks and Kimberly Clark, for among other creatures my eyes did see: a wildebeest, one of those old ladies who can bake shortbread cookies as she walks, her petticoats lifting and giving off an odor, two hundred orphans, a punning drunk (Who ties his shoes with a hangman's noose? The devil. Who ties his shoes with worms? The wackos), kids with lipstick making up mushrooms, poor puppeteers using the designs on their sweaters for scenery, Zeppelin whalers, trees-tall-tall-that-make-your-glasses-fall, a shirt with a paper airplane for a collar, a foreigner masturbating as he makes out shapes in the clouds, three hundred more orphans, a functionary who sports shoes above his size to step on even more cockroaches, a harlot crowned queen after retrieving a straw hat from the sand, a monk who has intercepted already three thrown cherries with his hand, a flying fish posed on King Rieseby's ring, a two-millimeter Hippopotamus, a businessman who wears his youngest daughter's braid for a tie, a lovebird who finds all this laughable, a throng that chops down the trees-tall-tall-that-make-your-glasses-fall to build bunkbeds for an orphanage of two, three, eight and up to seventy floors, a blue Masai, a church mouse with a church organ, a cat with little rhinoceros horns, a giant with clay tiles instead of hair, a staircase in place of a nose, the same gap through which he breathes and down which he hurls himself, monkeys and more monkeys, monkeys whose faces are threes.

All this there was and much more. Which is why I couldn't believe that Shanks, obsessed as he was with reducing everything to a single principle, would not repudiate that rabble. If even I experienced vertigo. That is to say, I did not rule out that the throng might be host to beauty, but, if so, what were you, wherein did predilection remain? Without the use of your formula, could one attain the beautiful?

And time and again I censored myself, telling myself: there is no truth in movement; a moving thing cannot be loved, it is but a guise. Disguised as movement, movement stands still. Finally, dizzy and discombobulated I fell at the feet of the merrymaking. Until Clark arrives:

> –Exposito, forget your footprints already. The moment is now. The senses are but brushes for fleshing out the flower. Pencils draw not what they are, but the color of time.

> –I don't want to! I want to wear footprints that match my shoe size, the ones I was wearing that day when I was happy. I've got to find them!

And as Clark walked off, Shanks waved in his hand a gingko biloba leaf and began to lead the throng. Two days into the decent, the procession made camp in a clearing at the foot of the mountains. The place was lovely, situated between lakes into which the river, so thick there, emptied, the river which was a bed of flowing blonde hair. There stood a half-ruined palace, a few alleys promulgated by ivy, and an old church with a cylindrical belltower resembling a flute. In short order, a fast-moving train makes its way down the abandoned track that the Sherpa and I had auscultated, our fear rising as the wall of a kibbutz goes up, rising with all the accumulated sleep, and a soaring tower of bunk beds is erected in which we orphans would sleep.

CHAPTER 7. FOUNDING OF THE KIBBUTZ NAMED THE ADORATION

Because they won me over: if each of us longed for a happy past, all of us holding hands and holding our breath would bring about a progressive era.

Thus was the Kibbutz inaugurated; the first name we gave it was Aurora, then later the Adoration.

For a few days even I forgot to die for beauty or to diffuse my origins in the kaleidoscopic. For a few days, truly, I forgot even you, enthusiastically surrendering to all kinds of performative concerns, ecologists, and tightrope walkers with whom we orphans trained.

We were going to do it together. Nothing would be left out: perfumes, threshing floors, colors, myths. For example, the goal was to return the seasons to a natural order until each was governed by a primary color. Shanks said he'd seen it happen before: he took the skeleton of an old bicycle, set it beside the wheat thresher, and, quite simply, pedaled. Right away, that thousand-year-old, wheel-shaped thresher made of giant stones creaked and began to spin just like a merry-go-round.

–Watch out for the column! Watch out for the column!

During all this, Kimberly Clark disseminated his theory on the naturalization of history:

–Everything to this point has been a conflict between supply and demand –and he prophesied a kind of advent in which supply would be forever relegated while demand would be satisfied hermaphroditically.

Though Armitage Shanks enjoyed greater success coloring in these theories with metaphysical notions:

–In the beginning was the offering. A worm in the form of a wheel with the possibility of another animal passing through its rings. That same God was, and is, a captive beast. But we are on the move, we will set him free. And one day we will live in peace, and wounds and sexes will cauterize dans le Siécle des Cercles.

Just then, he raised his arms slowly and, pressing his fingertips together, formed a circle above his head. Next, fixing his gaze upon the throng and with a voice that seemed other than his own, he shouted:

–Ooooooooooooooom!

The throng, not grasping his meaning, started lining up before him and mimicking his gesture like a legion of ballerinas: "Ooooom! Ooooooooooooooom!"

It was thus the worm in the form of a wheel became a symbol of the movement, while the encircled arms motion was turned into its official greeting. Yes, in the beginning, they all did it. And yes, admittedly, so did I.

What I did not know then was that we would have to fight for such peace, for any peace. I stood content before those symbols. And even the Sherpa, who was becoming suspicious, found himself admiring the castle of vertical fireworks, taking part in sack races, and winning a contest whose trophy was a truffle. He looked happy again. All appeared well.

The only holdout was a chattering. What's making that sound?

CHAPTER 8. GREYHOUND WITH CONE COLLAR AND NOBLE WITH RUFF CONTEMPLATE VANISHED COUNTRYSIDE

–Coming to you on the mic...chattering teeth! –joked Clark.

And when they flung open the door, what we saw startled us. Just as a pirate captain has his hook, so had the fellow a candle-holder in place of a palm, with one candle already there, dripping into his open hand. Sobabyette, as he was called, smelled of hair and nails, smelled of laudanum. With his lone useful hand, he was playing Couperin's *La convalescente* on the harpsicord. Meanwhile the hems and embroidery of his blouse were yellowing like Calla flowers or the anuses of swans.

There beside Sobabyette, the last of his military forces, a nutcracker doll with a bayonet and a painfully red uniform who was writing to him in a notebook:

–Highness, who are these men? The devil has come to nest in this valley! –And his teeth chattered from fear.

–See –said Clark –a classic case, our man operating within the equation of the old regime, the toboggan where the devil waits for you at the bottom to snatch you by the legs. Tell me, fearful man, how did you manage to stay hidden?

Sobabyette set down the harpsicord, blew out the candle in his hand, and spoke:

–You want to get rid of me, but this is my house, these are my dogs, and this is my collection of blown glass. Here I was conceived and here, within a forest of widowed nurses, in an intimate throb of fabric, was I born; here vertebra upon vertebra I grew. And look there – he gestured toward the garden with his candle whisps – in that alcove where my grandfather peed a yellow rose bush has arisen.

He gripped me by the arm and whispered in my ear:

–Despite what I say I know you understand me, that you will save me. You yourself want to die for beauty. We are near; look –and he showed me his ear– the inheritance from my grandfather, Narcissus' ear bones turned into the mechanism for a music box. Like me, you detest a world dispersed down causal tributaries. You are pure disruption. Look there at what your friends are up to; their lanterns going deep into Eden. Stop this insanity. The countryside is me, so said my uncle, King XIV –And then, adopting a seductive tone: –Come with me, I won't steal your toys.

–You are mistaken, Sir Count –Shanks interrupted–, what you see are lightning bolts in Thy Birth Forest, the revered site from which all came and to which all…he stopped himself.

Sobabyette to the Sherpa:

–Boy, do you understand they are going to take you away from your mentor?

The child's gaze glanced off mine, mine off Shanks's, Shanks's off

Clark's.

   –Is it true? –I asked.

Shanks took me by the shoulder:

   –Dearest Exposito, help is needed at the Kibbutz ovens, bread doesn't bake itself. But all this is temporary, your Sherpa will continue to assist you. You must not hold him back. Nor prevent him from going to school with the other boys. Would you press your hand upon the earth which hosts the seed? Would you leave it like that all spring?

   –No, no I don't agree…–But how to reason it out. The Sherpa could not be my adsum, for I knew not how to instruct him, nor could he hand his childhood over to me. Besides, he'd grown suspicious.

   –Are these men evil, Master?

   –Stay calm, Juan Boy –I answered. Though I was struggling to do the same; Shanks tied up all the dogs and Clark snatched the bayonet from the Nutcracker. –But, friends, all this is nothing more than a wax museum!

The Nutcracker could not stop his chattering, so I put a sock in his mouth. Then we retreated to our assigned bunks.

The following day, the Sherpa was no longer with me.

CHAPTER 9. *THE GAP*
(HE TOLD ME – THE PEACH)

I climbed down from my bunk, number nineteen, and went right away to ask where the Kibbutz ovens were and if they had seen him, the Sherpa. But I found only the Nutcracker, Sobabyette's little red soldier, and he would not answer those questions. Instead:

> –Listen here, I'm going to tell you something. If you help us, I'll help you –he jotted in his notebook.

Yes, I replied, I would help them. So he told me. He spoke to me of an autistic philosopher. He lives at the top of the old belltower: the Philosopher writes on a typewriter, seated at a table, an immense banquet table whose far end is lost in fog.

He longs to write something, yes, something, but what.

> ~You cannot capture the moment; your hand gets bruised in its revolving door. I dream a chimeral hand, all arrayed with fingers, a crab-hand, a star-hand, a compass-rose-index-ring-and-heart-hand. I dream this hand because mine is nettled by the real, for example, a peach, a pomme, the pommel on a door.

He says your past exists not; not your present, either. That he had tried everything. And nothing. That he has employed "methods." Not even then. The-Iron-Chain-in-Bloom-*Non-Stop-Show.* That

he had tried up there. He had tried even there. He could recall the sound of ice in a glass but could not replicate it. Then there was the pubic triangle, arrow pointing always to hell. And the train: *mind the gap, please,*
mind
the gap.

The cleft between language and its adoration.

Please, please, keep clear, do not obstruct the doors.

He says that forms come out of him; he describes how he draws them from his mouth just like the fire-eater, manipulating his mouth with his fingers to create the form for what he's thinking. And those are his words. Yet in vain. For they are still phantoms.

And he cannot remember life, having turned it into the past or into snoring; never to remerge, for the seamstress enters not through the eye of her needle, nor a rotten apple through a luscious apple. Therefore, the fundamental question: if I tell this to no one and "this" happens, did this even happen?

He laments that his sentences go on disintegrating with no return. That he reviews them and finds no grammatical error. Yet still they crumble. He tells stories with no end, like the one the Nutcracker jotted down:

> the little bridges
> the little men cross
> with hands in pockets
> above little rivers
> with hands in pockets

He told me this, the Nutcracker, yes. He said the Philosopher even gets sick at the table. That he never raises a hand to stop them from serving him and that wine runs down his hand and dyes his nails. That the girls laugh. Except one, called Ancila, I believe…

I bid him halt his pen:

> –Ancila? The Seamstress of Thy Birthplace? She came to my aid!

The Nutcracker shrugged his shoulders with a wood-like creaking and concluded his tale. The autistic Philosopher no longer goes out, no longer visits The-Iron-Chain-in-Bloom-*Non-Stop-Show*. If he needs something, he tosses a bag on a rope out the tower window, a sickly kite. But writing, oh yes, he writes to no end:

I have analyzed his language, theme, and rhyme, and have determined that his syntax tells the story of an adoration.

CHAPTER 10. THE SEAMSTRESS ENTERS (NOT) THROUGH THE EYE OF THE NEEDLE

I had not left the Hamlet for the purpose of establishing a kibbutz. Of course not: no matter how deep my involvement had been, how much deeper my involvement would grow.

I left the Nutcracker scribbling his last words. I took the Hallway of the Sisters and after it a subjective path through the cornfield, a passage neither narrow nor wide, but that your feet would stretch like a pea does its pod, a foot in a sock. Later I arrived at the station with the train to the mountains. *Keep clear, do not obstruct the doors.* Just one station.

The-Iron-Chain-in-Bloom-*Non-Stop-Show* was a cloth Chinese dragon abandoned in a parking lot; perhaps a holdover of ancient folklore or a dubious gift from a neighboring city. The thing to know is that now it hosts in its interior the total prostitution of the environment. It was fitting that Shanks should compare the racking in the dragon's guts to the roar of decomposition and decline of tradition.

On each tooth of the dragon, a letter:

T-O T-H-E G-I-R-L-S

I entered and my glasses fogged over. It was my blushing. Curtain after curtain; some girls are mouse-faced; others are mouse-faced. As I passed by, a few made the encircled arms motion, others did not. More curtains. One peels back suddenly, and I'm snatched, I'm dragged into an inner room. Darkness at first; then:

–Exposito! You here? What a happy sight you are! Who is Armitage Shanks? Men came looking for us at the Mountain Hamlet, Thy Birthplace; they brought us to this secret valley. They brought my mother, too. She's sick. They, they screamed at us, shrieking our names, syllable by syllable. They've dragged me, here, you see. Scandalous. She stares right at me: –And the boy? Where is the boy?

–Ancila, how are you? I have so many questions for you…

–Where is my brother Juan?

–Your brother…is fine –I lied, since for the first time it dawned on me that, in my obsessiveness, night had fallen without inquiring about the ovens or the school, without reporting his disappearance: –Your brother works in the Kibbutz now; they treat him well, better than me.

 –Is that why you were looking for a seeing-eye squire?

–Well, he's not a seeing-eye squire. –And despite having lost all faith in what I was saying, I continued: We are building a destiny, and you, will you help me?

–I should help you? Me help you?

–I was told a tale about an autistic philosopher, who I think you know, and what happened to him is exactly what happened to me. –Disgusted, Ancila turned pale, but I continued: You know? I no longer think of "the girl," but of "a girl." I prefer now to remember her when a lavender scent blows across the mountain, even though she never used any perfume. But it's better this way, for time has imparted to her laces a foul smell, a swamp-like smell.

Ancila sat up in her bed. She was looking downcast. After a minute, she lifted her gaze:

–Has nothing I've said mattered to you?

I turned her words over and over in my head. I sat down beside her:

–Tomorrow I'll ask what they want from you and why they've brought you here, I swear. No harm can come from it. I'll help you; I believe I have a role to play in this story.

Timorously, I drew near Ancila and kissed her face, yet before leaving:

–Just one question: if I tell this to no one and "this" happens, did this even happen?

Ancila shook her head and, without looking at me, recited from memory:

–The snow melts yet it is white. A knot may lose its form but never its function. On a given day you may shut a door but not the doorway. If a door opens, it remains forever open. Rain disappears, but one can look forever on the desert with a silver mask.

–My Ancila, I count on your words. I'll be back for more.

The metro doors.
Please, do not obstruct the doors.
Do not abstract the doors.
Keep clear. Please. Please.

The door in spring puts forth a flower. In summer, the flower fruits a pommel. In fall, your hand is mashed by the pommel. In winter, doors have no pommels, nor can they be opened.

CHAPTER 11. IT WAS THE SIXTH DAY OF
THE RED SEASON

The following day, Armitage Shanks and Kimberly Clark sat on bunk thirty-nine and had a heated argument over the status of orphans: should all human beings be included – Clark – or only the race from our ever more beloved Thy Natal Forest – Shanks?

Later, Clark raised the notion that the Kibbutz's growth would fatten the Congress; the youth and recent arrivals would complete the circle and cause the hemicycle to grow into a cycle and a circus. In short, the history of thought transmuted into the present of an obsession. Predictably, speaking in circles pleased Shanks; the heavy steps of divergence compared to the greased rhythm of the One. Marvelous. The House of Representatives would grow into a tower and, from its heights, the flower of a flag would unfurl. But what flag? That was for a later dialogue. Besides, there was still the other tower to celebrate, the one of bunks, already two hundred leaps taller than the church belltower. Indeed, some swore it was the only human edifice visible from space. It is not odd, therefore, that the highest bunks would for long stretches be snowed under with the orphans having to sleep with their socks on.

Shanks was wide-smiling, already imagining the future House packed with ecstatic heads, the faces of the Adoration, silent as stones in the walls of a well:

–Come here, Exposito! Out of the snow and from their

continents, one day forests shall emerge. Can't you hear the Adoration drawing near?

But I would no longer be silenced. It was my turn. Like a gale, I hurled my admonitions:

–No, Armitage, I won't hear it. It is you who will hear me: Where is the Sherpa? Why have you taken him? And I want the truth. And moreover, tell me exactly…Where do I fit in here?

–Dear poet, the Revelation requires you!

–Armitage, with each successive evangelist the Revelation fades. The Revelation is not our pet, nor can it stay here with us. Don't you get it? I don't want the fish that has eaten its tail, but one that through an aesthetic effort pushed further to swallow its fins, eyes, and mouth. The one who disappears. I believe in the death of the future world. But anyway, that's not what I want to talk about just now...

Just then a chattering compelled me to turn my gaze toward the threshold. With great effort the little Nutcracker was dragging the Sherpa's small, heaving body. I rushed to take him in my arms.

It was the Sixth Day of the Red Season, summer. I had such goosebumps that I grew feathers.

Today I'm not sure how, but I remained unruffled then, I did not stand by. And it's a fact that, initially, I was able to save his life. Without medical support nor oxygen in a kibbutz whose apparatuses were geared toward a single purpose – the formation of the Worm Brigade – I decided to bring the boy to the palace of Sobabyette. Once there I grabbed a bauble of blown glass and brought it near him. I hadn't entirely miscalculated, for while the sphere was reflecting his massively swollen nose, the boy managed a long, deep breath.

But it wasn't enough. Two hours later he died, surrounded by glass baubles, either clouded from his breath or smashed in my desperation. It was the Sixth Day of the Red Season. I lowered my head and rested my brow on the Sherpa's lifeless little arm.

CHAPTER 12: THE DEVIL WALKS BACKWARDS

I found an envelope under my pillow. I had returned to my bunk, wanting to prepare for the wake. And to hide. I was stricken. I held the envelope in my hands until cold sweat unstuck the glue. It was a letter from Clark and Shanks. Rather concise: it entrusted me with the design of a pantheon. One consecrated to Childhood.

I fastened the button where the Sherpa would never again stick out his head. I looked at the little sleeves Ancila had stitched on either side of the chest and, with a lump in my throat, cut them off with scissors. I hid my head inside the fur coat and stayed that way, sitting on my bunk, legs dangling in space, hands in pockets, eyes peering through the cut-off sleeves.

The commotion came from downstairs, from the news I supposed.

–The Devil has come to nest in this valley! announced a leaflet that arrived from the air.

I stuck out my head. I stuck out my hands. I blushed my glasses. This time for no reason, for it was only the Nutcracker:

–Not one Devil here, Nutcracker, not any Devil.

–Yes, there is, there is– he wrote between tremors: – One morning, a spider swung from the cemetery into My Lord's hands. He, believing it was a daisy and conjuring up past loves, plucked off the spider's legs: she loves me, she loves me not, she loves me...; but I know it was the Devil asking himself if he should nest here: nest, no, nest, no, nest, no, nest, no.

–Okay? That's it: "no nest;" you said it. There are eight legs, he won't nest, he won't come; the Devil does not exist.

–Of course! The Devil walks backwards, talks backwards, counts in reverse! – he wrote – Satan is already among us! He made me distract you yesterday when you went looking for your Sherpa. The chattering became unbearable, and several orphans gathered below:

–The Demon? The Demon!!! Hahaha!

I rose and conducted myself to the wake. As I passed, those gathered made the idiotic encircled arms motion, though some fell over laughing. Even so, I faced them. I argued that our loss in fact opened a path to a gain, "this time truly and completely interior," as the poet said, and that with shards of memory one might relate in an improved sequence the tale of the lost one, transforming basic experiences into feats and the beloved into the hero of an Icelandic epic. I compared poets to moles, boring through the earth, crossing Mohorovičić's discontinuity and then Dahm's and then Gutenberg's until reaching the planet's core, fire, intuition. And that is where the body of the boy...

Suddenly, something thrown from the crowd smashed against my spine: "Psssst", Fooooour-eyes!" "Weeeeeeirdo!" and even "Harlequiiin!" but I dared not turn around. I left off mid-peroration. I curled my body around my daydreams:

~Haha, but you really don't get it? Kid, we don't call that a headboard, we call it a tombstone.

CHAPTER 13. DREAM OF THE BLOOD AND THE TWO CHAMBERLAINS

The Nutcracker and I were holding vigil for the little boy. At some point, my eyelids closed on me, and then I was visited by the spider Sobabyette had torn the legs from. He spoke to me, saying:

> ~I'm alive, I'm alive. Insects dance lying down, they don't die, they can't die no matter how many legs are torn from them; they wheel their legs, they take their time. I take my time, I will not become extinct; as you live so shall I live, I shall live so the possibility of yes and no exists, for I am love and no love, sense and nonsense. In a single point I am ground and abyss; I am Schrödinger's cat, who marks his territory, pissing on the no within the yes, the death within life. All save the word of man am I, and I shall reign through the signs of signs.

But I could not listen, I could not listen, I opened my eyes, stretched and said it was high time to begin the procession.

Neither Clark nor Shanks attended the ceremony. And if, oppressed by their guilt, they were not there, who better than Sobabyette to perform the office. My new friend arrived attired in a blouse the hems of which had yellowed like Calas or the anuses of swans.

I asked him about the meaning of the young dead, their venomous beauty. He responded:

–There are alternative heavens, angels like eight-year-old children who never leave their orphanage beds.

I fashioned a cross, transversally sewing the sleeves Ancila had made, the boy's sister, the ones she had appended to my fur coat and which I had just cut off. And while flowers confer quiet and devotion, I thought of something a little different. I purchased some fish. Burying their tails in the ground like roots, their two fins were as leaves and their heads resembled corollas. Later, I opened their mouths one-by-one so they could cross pollinate, maybe with a little help from the flies. It was a small tribute to the boy's imagination, which I was allowed to underscore. At the very end, we hoisted a flag of shooting stars.

I felt drained, sad for the little boy and of necessity impelled to remember you to overcome my fatigue. I climbed into my bunk, number nineteen. I closed my eyes, buried the two seeds. I dreamed: a castle filled with stairs ascended and descended by chamberlains with bowls filled with the blood of the ephemeral king. I watch them. I believe they are headed for the Courtyard. Indeed, there, into an enormous basin, they pour the blood from bloodletting procedures. One chamberlain tells me I must remember, must remember what I love before the king's blood coagulates. I try to remember, to remember, to remember but get nervous and go blank. Now all the chamberlains are in the Yard, surrounding me:

~Too late! they say. Too late! The king's blood has already jellied!

Then, bending over the basin, laughing we take handfuls of that blood and fling it at each other like snow:

~We are free! We are free!

And under my breath:

~Such gelatinous darkness...

CHAPTER 14. NOW DO YOU UNDERSTAND ME?

–No! You shall not leave the Kibbutz! Exposito, you must change. Today, without further delay, in the Plaza, we are going to set fire to your Diogenes syndrome for all the world to see.

September's first gust had shaken the tree shadows. I was next to Shanks, the two of us sitting in his bunk, number thirty-nine. The man landed his words right in my wound. For, truthfully, I could understand the attachment to objects, the parts, the fractions, individuating each, and us along their lines; all for having led love to the place of...illness. Even without suffering it, who has not caught a glimpse of madness, which, really, if looked at from a distance, sits just behind sanity, as another syndrome.

Just then, Shanks, who was amusing himself with a box of matches, sparked one on my brow, scorching my ruminations. Then he blew out the first, pulled another out, and, without sparking it, held the match up to me:

–Watch, Exposito. – With his thumb he covered the matchstick, leaving the head barely visible.

–Right here is pure fire, but no such combustion will happen. We are not ready, all things in all dimensions would burn. – Then he ran his index finger down the matchstick and declared: –Though this news may be of some use to us. This is how the temple columns grow, not toward God, not toward God, my friend, but away from God, moving away from His fire. And preserving it. You understand me? This is what I didn't tell you; it's too late for anything else. There is one death preceding Death. Now you know, this is my true poem, a nothing formed out of men orphaned through and through.

You already suspect this; language is like a chicklet held in the mouth for a while, a parody of nourishment. Bread nurtures us; the word bread celebrates that we are going to die.

That's why no one will stop me, not Sobabyette's devil nor Kimberly Clark. Nor you. Nothing will stop me, for I have no fear, I have nothing to lose. You understand? –he repeated– Are you coming with me? Recall that in abandoning the Mountain Hamlet you laid the first stone, awakening us. You were the first to deny the light: the fish swims not because there is water, but because it is fish. You spoke these words. And now you want to abandon me?!

I was speechless: ~One death there is preceding Death...~Too late...no, I didn't get it. And I could think of nothing to say. Who was this man? What was he after? And what was going to happen now? I said nothing and under his attentive, feverish gaze I searched for the ladder.

–Goodbye, Armitage, goodbye...

Through my head tumbled phrases like: homo homini lupus, or distorted in absurdity: columba columbae columba, lupus lupo columba, homo lupo ursus, etc. I climbed down. I climbed down the ladder. A half hour walk, the Hallway of the Sisters, the subjective path that functions like a peapod and, finally, the station with the train to the mountains. *Keep clear.*

CHAPTER 15. A DISAPPEARANCE WITH THE AROMA OF LAUDANUM

Getting off the train, I stumble upon a box of old toys and, next to it, a chipped birdhouse on whose little door you can still make out: "Cats are dumb!"

The message from the birds. I remembered your soul, its gestures. When something stirred you, you'd lift your chin emitting an "e" with a giggle, a giggle into which your molars snuck like stowaways. But those toys were abandoned. My perceptions anchored through a nervous-nostalgic system to your gestures. All destitute creatures slaked themselves with the shyness of a deer in the mirror of your conscience, to see in you their dignity reflected, to test their flotation devices, their weight, their crazy, far-fetched measure.

I drew closer. From the bottom of the box something gleamed. I reached down. It was the most beautiful bibelot of snow I'd ever beheld. A classic. A shiny black stone and, inside the glass, all alone, buried in snow, the miniature of a doll with scarf, carrot, and top hat; perfect as a Phidias sculpture: A snowman made from marble?

What could it be, why had it come my way, and, above all, the fact of its stillness. I've thought about these things quite a bit, the stillness of these things; words, expressions fallen from use and that someone by chance resuscitates. Does the archeologist make his home in the ruins? No, I think not, in other words, who would honestly go in there, or, better said, what was he really looking for? Wasn't I being a monster? I considered the example of Pompeii and it gave me goosebumps. I knew that the bodies of Vesuvius were not really bodies, bubbles of lava perhaps. Molds for an eruption. The outside in. The opposite of a sculpture. What a macabre and capricious thing, how frivolous of the elements to preserve an instant. That blast of energy and matter was so sorrowful that for my part I, without taking on some greater mysticism, could never call it love, not without some terrifying and oppositional exercise in nihilism. Unlike you.

That's why one day I said that you are your body, you are your body in full.

And, at the same time, my early childhood and the replacement one you brought me. The very stillness of all things. I sat upon the grass. And there I was absorbed. Until I felt it: a friendly warmth, a breath. What did you want to tell me? I turned. But found no one, only a faded dark brown getting lost within a hedge, a disappearance with the aroma of laudanum. I swallowed the knot in my throat and dropped into my left pocket, which already held the Sherpa's fingernails, the bibelot of snow. I bid goodbye to the rest of the toys and carried on my way.

CHAPTER 16. CLARK, SHANKS, CLARK, SHANKS, CLARK, SHANKS...

Back then, the silhouette of The-Iron-Chain-in-Bloom glinted in the distance. And the racking festivity of decomposition came literally to a sputtering boil. But what really caught my attention was the presence of a horse-drawn carriage; it was parked beside the head of the cloth dragon.

T-O T-H-E G-I-R-L-S

I entered and the lenses of my glasses fogged over. As always, my blushing. Curtain after curtain. Some frightened girls were making the encircled arms greeting.

–Oh, give it a rest! Where is Ancila Sternli? Tell me. Where is she?

–She's not here, she left, join the party.

A man took me by the arm:

~The whores are always six, crispy queens; look at them, simply lovely, girls spooked by the sight of themselves.

~No, don't touch me there, that's still my body! Sick little pig boy.

–But who took her? And to where? Tell me already!

Just then I was pushed further into the dragon, into a stom-ach-shaped saloon where a banquet was being served. At the harpsichord, to enliven the soiree...Sobabyette! With his candle-stick hand, he illuminates the keys; with the other, he plays *La convalescente*. But people keep right on speaking and eating. They seem to be friends of Sobabyette:

> ~We've already figured out the first major infrastructure improvement project; we will cover the roads with Persian rugs.

> ~But Augusto, the rugs are the skin of a vernal beast. It'll be too expensive!

Or simply:

> ~Have you noticed how narrow my head is? A woman's hat fits me fine.

As ever, I feared the diverse, for the form my admiration took entailed the taming of the world, in archiving it; but not like you, with your soul of hugs. Perhaps, I don't know, in place of the living spring, I would have preferred a solitary alchemy that left it stilled, mine, a frottage of spring.

But then, how precisely had I, a collector, come to speak in fixed ideas and train my thoughts in trusses? Why had I come to think that you had been messiah not of your world but of mine, and my love for you a tree leaning against the kiosk of my whims. And so, I drank and drank to get drunk and to make it through my vertigo.

Later, the notes Sobabyette had begun playing began to reverberate in my ears. Playing? Each pluck of the harpsichord reproduced the rattling of swords:

> ~Clark! Shanks! Clark! Shank! Clark! Shanks! Shanks! Clark! Shaaaaaaanks!

The whole party erupted in laughter. I stood:

> –Sobabyette! What is it you wish to say? No one is going to fight. Armitage had a bad day, that's all. We're friends.

But while everyone is laughing and the festival is erupting with feathers flying, lipstick, and desperation, I decide to leave, to board the train about to run over me. The path with the peapod function and the Hallway of the Sisters.

Arriving, my heart thumps faster than ever. However, everything appears to be in order. I take off my shoes to climb slowly to my bunk, number nineteen. And from up there I see them: Clark and Shanks. They are the only ones on the patio, having a good time practicing night tennis, a deeply relaxing game practiced with two hand mirrors, in which the moon's reflection is lobbed back and forth. Later, I watched them ever so quietly climb the ladder, to bunks seventeen and thirty-nine, respectively. I heard the sweet murmuring of soft mattresses and fell asleep thinking that fortunately Sobabyette's concerns were pointless.

CHAPTER 17. AN HOURGLASS DESERT

But Sobabyette did have a point; he had a point and had as well a collection of blown glass, silkworms, distilled laudanum, silver teaspoons and hourglasses, though, in the matter that concerns us, what mattered was his point. And when I turned to face the palace, I saw further down the path that they'd switched out the flag of shooting stars from the Sherpa's tomb; now the Worm waved. The cross had been pulled down and the fish felled. Behind me, bootheels clicking; it was the Worm Brigade, returning from a campaign. With them was a procession of men and women whom I identified as prisoners, for the dogs were barking, the dogs snatched from Sobabyette.

I picked up my pace.

After them came the clattering of leashes. After them came the clattering of pulleys and chains and screws. The demolition of the palace was already underway, the whole place having been filled with shattered glasses and scattered teaspoons.

–Come in, Exposito, come, take a seat.

–Sobabyette, you've got to get out of here!

–Don't be scared–he said, gazing skyward expectantly for one of the numbered horseman–, they will be long in arriving to the west wing. Tell me: when was it these straight, angular lines showed up, and all the clattering? And what is that? he asked pointing to a stoplight.

For Sobabyette knew of nothing beyond his palace and his garden, other palaces and other gardens, the interior of the horse-drawn carriage and the rooms of the The-Iron-Chain-in-Bloom, which he knew before it was called the *Non-Stop-Show*.

When I explained to him that it was a stoplight, he made a disgusted face: in the country, they didn't have machines and carriages had enough time to stop. Indeed, there had been in his world a fraternal relationship between things and their uses and, if the relationship came to be conventional, they all attended the convention, all celebrated the weddings. While this was the way, he reasoned, the earth never became contaminated, and the nature of man was Nature.

Just then a memory of you came back to me, of the grief abandoned objects had caused you and how these objects, vivified within your joyful animism, lined up before your gaze so you could bestow on them a task, or, better said, a sensibility: old houses, empty stores that wound up shuttered, dirty dogs resting their chins on your palm, trashed furniture, the ancient floors of plazas, smooth as the skin of an elderly Parisian lady. Once upon a time a girl said, "God save the queen of the hive," just before she swallowed a spoonful of honey.

My gaze fell to the earth and Sobabyette, unable to guess of who or of what I was thinking, but perceiving my misery, felt himself to be in good company:

> –This is why I have no desire to leave this place. You understand me now, yes? I was born here, here I grew, vertebrae upon vertebrae, here was I a child, when the marble steps still undulated. Let's face it, between these broken walls I will die.

–Sobabyette–, the past does not exist, though it persists.

–Tu quoque!? Time is a state of mind! Look at my collection of clocks. Where does the sand in the hourglass come from? Do you think it's desert sand, that it's barren? The sand from my Auteuil clocks? No, Exposito, no it is not. Come, let's cheer with the clocks while everything winds down and they leave us in peace to our teensy-weensy past.

My friend freed the clocks from their little wooden gallows and, after raising our glasses, we got completely wasted on that sand. Then, somehow a chattering managed to rise over the murmur of the engines; it was the little Nutcracker dragging a sack full of all the stuff he was able to salvage: the collection of silkworms, the dog collars, a bottle of laudanum, a few remaining teaspoons, glasses still intact...ah, a bustle built by Eiffel, the architect!

–Bravo, Nutcracker!

And so, Sobabyette, who had thought all was lost, consented in his wasted state to leave the palace. The cranes pecked at the statues and columns and though the volutes were fitted with boxing gloves, they could do nothing to fend off ruination. Already devastated was the field where once in place of wheat spears sprouted royal peacock plumes, blue bread for those with blue blood. Neither ranches nor gardens would remain; in fact, a highway would be run right through the middle of the China vase. In a state of resignation, my new friend contemplated the horizon and the old flute-shaped belltower. Then he bid me goodbye, gifting me the last of his hourglasses.

–You might need it.

And I thought not, but he thrust the hourglass into my left pocket where, beside the Sherpa's fingernails and the bibelot I'd found, it went on counting sand.

The horse-drawn carriage waited. I watched him drive off as I grew more alone.

CHAPTER 18. MY LITTLE VENICE

I climbed the ladder to bunk seventeen, Kimberly Clark's.

–Why did you spit on me?

–I wanted to give you a kiss, but you were way over there. You're a traitor, you helped the son of a bitch escape. You don't know his lineage, the kings, the ones who make peace pacts on horseback. The horseback peace perpetuating the war.

–Hello, Mr. Payback, I hardly helped him at all…I seek only to get lost on my own path, which is a paralysis, like his.

–A poet, a four-eyes, a harlequin. You're the one who taught us freedom, you know? The fish swims not because there is water, but because it is fish. You said it, the day we couldn't stop staring at our hands. And now look, you're making a mess, getting sand all over the sheets. And you reek of laudanum!

Speaking with Clark wasn't going to be easy. Shanks and he were analogs, primarily in their modes of disagreement. They were like two books that had yellowed side-by-side, shat on by the same fly and so tightly pressed together that their plots and characters wound up merging.

–You and your beauty, you and your immobility, the zephyr in the bobbin of the convent's lathe. Polluted, polluted... and failed! That's you, that's Exposito. And you know what this is? A pair of scissors, yes.

He proceeds to cut out a few yellowed pages, ones that looked familiar:

–Let's see:

Whales are shadows of clouds
that also bear storms;
stirred up thunderclaps
they squawk with language.

Come, come, what's this?

The stone is slower light...

...the Sultan in his harem enumerates and enamors.

Did you write this? This is yours, Exposito? It's filth! And this, too? This, really? Did you call the toilet My Little Venice!?

–No! That's not true, you're making things up! Give me back those pages! –we wrestled on the mattress –Anyway the poems are only a hobby, what I want is to di...

The poems flew into the air. Shredded.

–So, tell me, does what's happening here mean nothing to you? Of course, Exposito, the genie from your lamp grants wishes, but he does not administer them. That's what policy is for. What's more, a world without causes or consequences plugs God back into his lost habitat. You speak of love, too, but you don't love, you regurgitate ghosts. Listen up, until now time has been but a souvenir: hourglasses, cuckoos, bibelots. But this will change, now's your chance! Just do it, yonder is a cesspool for your ectoplasms; help me save the women and the men, the elders and the young.

And I gazed below: demolished palace, bewildered people, machines and more machines, soldiers and solitude, the Worm Brigade.

–Has no helpful thought occurred to you? Think! –And think I did. I thought that my head was a glasses-wearing meteorite approaching earth that, prior to impact, left its glasses on the little night table of the moon: –No, really? You've got nothing to say? Didn't think so.

I had lost myself inside me but pulled myself together:

–So does the Sherpa's death mean nothing to you?

–Are you still coming with that? Childhood is the Olympus of your autism, the dwarfism of your decadence. You're disgusting.

And when wanting to cut short our little chat I sought out the ladder's rungs, I could feel under the bedspread not a mattress, but...

–A suitcase?

Clark wide-smiled:

–Yes, friend, I'm leaving, but I'm not abandoning the
struggle, the struggle continues beyond here. Now per-
haps Shanks is more our enemy than your count with the
candle hand. If you want, you can come with us, if you
change. It's still possible you'll prove useful, not with your
friendship songs or umbilical songs, but with stories, true
stories: Write the first novel of the Revolution! –And in
my hand, he placed an envelope.

–Make up a novel you say? No, never, we must stay awake,
always awake, looking death in the eye, "like parched larks
at the mirage," the poet said. –Though I thought, too, of
my eagerness to escape, my innumerable siestas...

Clark grabbed the suitcase and beat me down the ladder:

–See you later, weirdo!

Watching him go, I repeated to myself: ~There go the rivals,
headed to a place where they shall become still greater rivals,
carrying the tools to fashion themselves into inveterate rivals.

CHAPTER 19. FIRST NOVEL OF THE REVOLUTION

There are also flowers I did not give you, some of them with all the colors. Yes, the world existed, but within it no things remained, as within you they remained, as you within your body. If you were to build a house, it would be by setting each stone in the space corresponding to its form, foreshortening with no cement and with no adobe or anything extra that would have to be stuffed in sacks, bottles, series, or lexicons. No, only correspondences. In other words, the earth existed and you existed. You, like an agriculture.

All this was swirling around in my head when I reached my bunk and discovered a brown dog laying there, abandoned. It gave off the same laudanum scent as the apparition from a few days back. Laudanum?

> –Who are you? –I asked. But he didn't budge. Who are you? If you don't turn around, I'll never know who you are.

Slowly he obeyed. Kanguno was not a marsupial canid like any other, as I used to tell people to justify my name for him or to explain why no one ever petted him. Nor did he have rosebush thorns along his legs; it was only that with mud his short hairs had been plastered to look like thorns. In short, he was not a special breed, not a greyhound, not a hunting hound, just an old dog whose fang showed even when he closed his mouth. Which was why he had not been conscripted. Instead of just saying that,

I invented the fable into which the idea of dog was not assimilable, for in general I prefer a circumlocution to a barebones reality. In short, in the welcoming space of your gaze, I made plays on words, aeronautic designs for Noah's Ark.

I reasoned that if I wanted to keep him, I should keep him hidden. But Kanguno was quite docile. And when night fell or dangerous sorts drew near, he kept still as a bedside table and consented to my draping some skirting over him in a way that would draw no attention. For who knows how to classify a hairy table with rosebush thorns? No one. Thus, he would remain invisible. Kanguno would be mine.

Happy to no longer be alone, I opened the envelope that Clark had left. I read. It was a sketch for a realist novel. And surprisingly, I thought: Why not give it a go? It went against my principles, yet...my principles? Where had they gone? Might my narrative bring me some minimal status?

And so I began filling up pages. The preterit is important, I said, yes, that's right, the preterit is important. And I used it. But problems ran rampant. I knew that I was floundering when I wrote to salvage images and from them derived a theme both subsidiary and forced. Because it was absurd for Sherlock Holmes to uncover the invisible man simply by turning over a jar full of ants. It made no sense. Not any more so than him cracking the case by casting a Zeppelin's shadow onto a Ouija board. Just because I happened to like Zeppelins and Ouija boards? Not a chance, of course not.

I switched to dirty realism. Brutal gangsters, vendettas, blood and guts oozing along like russet amoebas. But what was it all about? I had not overlooked the following: that in order to denounce evil one needs to express and then, for a split second, tolerate it; and when this evil no longer frightens, up the ante, feed more firewood into the earthly pits of hell.

And yet the height of absurdity was a book in which the inmates of a concentration camp were rats. There was even a scene where the rat Aldo, mid-escape, says to his brothers: "Speak no Polish nor wiggle your whiskers even if something smells strongly of cheese." Yes, I get it, it sounds like a cheesy joke, but I was searching for another vantage onto that which, in the end, should not be novelized.

My final and perhaps most successful attempt was the autobiography of a young man in the middle of a life crisis, committed to writing a book call *The Adoration.* But my own end I knew not, nor did I know the end of my book, and, moreover, seeing reflected in its pages both a world and an approach to life condemned to extinction, I started to scare myself.

And so I wrote no further, pulled the lace curtain over Kanguno and I, and cast down to the bunks below pages and more pages and a pen.

I curled the cot over, closed my eyes, and contemplated the stars.

CHAPTER 20. BOW OR ARROW?

The Velcros of autumn were already worn out, the Yellow Season, when, on the following day, Kanguno and I left the Kibbutz behind us. But as escapes are treacherous going, the first thing we encountered was a forest in which each fir, instead of standing, was hung from the stars by a noose, brushing and brushing the forest floor as they swayed. After a moment's hesitation, I took Kanguno in my arms and started pushing against trunks, which ceded passage with a creaking as of the rigging of a ship's jib. Then terror came over us, for in this hanging forest if the wind picked up one could easily be crushed to death. In the end I don't know if it was from our terror or lack of know-how, but we lost our way and emerged not far from where we started out, in the place where the already full-bodied river emptied, the river that was a bed of flowing blonde hair.

I was startled then by the vision of a shaved-headed women, shabbily dressed, who lay upon on the shore. I hid my head inside my fur coat. Yet:

–You let them take my brother away! –she shouted pummeling my chest with her slender fists.

I think for a minute I stopped breathing. Certainly, my fish, my famous fish, was suffocating out of water.

–Ancila, I didn't leave, I couldn't have known what was coming. I'm sorry....what can I say...

–Well, what's your next move? Kimberly Clark is stock-piling rockets and basilisks. At the very least you can save yourself. My godfather and I want to flee.

–And your mother? Then your mother...

–And I will give to them a name everlasting that none shall cut away (Isaiah 24:3)

–You're referring to the arts?

–Behold the family violin. Still, it knows how to lead me to their doors, near to her, to them, to Him.

–To their doors? Well, I don't want to get invited to a threshold. If I enter, it will be on my own two feet.

Ancila stepped back from me and replied:

–The forest is a clock in which suddenly the wolf brings down the doe. But only God sets the clock on time.

–And if he's running late? If God forgets? Don't you see how what you're saying will result in your abandonment?

She seemed beside herself:

–When I hear him coming, I raise up my heart and eyes in my hands and he gives himself to me. Night love. And at dawn's first light, before he leaves me, a word of mine is lit with his fire. The fate of that elusive word is the very same that befell the deer in the wildfire: to spread the fire. Then the geyser of the poem gushes out. These are only words, but the barren land has been impregnated with his image. Like an arrow from my vocal cords, the enamored air is loosed.

–And if nothing flies forth? Your God buries us along with his creation. Listen here, my intelligence will become a school of fish and it will devour his face. They will devour thy face, Lord! For I shall climb atop my soul and cast myself into the void. And one day I will go on another date with her, "in summer's blue afternoons," until we arrive to the end of the end. "To die like parched larks at the mirage." Did you know that skeletons have been discovered orbiting the planet, birds that were calcined from soaring into the atmosphere?

–The dead floating on planets without gravity? Antigone of the moon? Horrific! Yet you don't even believe your own story, so why keep repeating yourself?! Will you turn out worse than them? Go get your house in order, the story is coming to its end.

–What house, tell me? Icarus burns his nest! –I began to shout, and the echo of my own, rather ludicrous sentences, made me blush.

Ancila did not say goodbye. She set off through the forest. A screeching violin and aching trees followed. The last Velcro of autumn fell.

CHAPTER 21. THE TRACKS SPEED ALONG

What made you different than the rest? Exactly who were you? I'll repeat, you were your love, and when recalling those early days, often I thought of our high school, one desk beside the other. You had sketched the Jacobson schema for functional communications; your receiver had a large ear, your transmitter a large mouth, and the code was a carnation.

Where did I first meet you? There is no longer anyone who remembers. In the opera, they say, "Un dì, felice, eterea, mi balenaste innante," in other words, you crossed right in front of me. So I stood still and you passed by? Yet that cannot be; let's call it a tragedy. Indeed, for the intention is to restore the cosmic order to its denouement, to return to the exposition, this time without plots compromising essences. Must everyone die to attain equilibrium? Well put, this is a tragedy. Nonetheless, following Aristotelian norms, I, hero, should have taken the first step, I would not stand still. *Poetics* states it clearly: the actant is fate's victim, yet he is an actant; he is the one who initiates the plot, even if only with a flourish, even if only with a breath. In such a way that–taking up paper, pen, and ruler–we speak of two causes that cross transversely in the following manner:

I→ ↑   or else   I → ↓
   you   you

or instead, never   ↑ ← I   nor   ↓ ← I
             you   you

No grand act is required, just a small step. One can see that you start to move, and I, who have yet to catch sight of you, begin to walk. Bah. Whatever. What matters is data, the treasure map. For where would such an encounter take place? Only in an open field, that is to say, in the countryside–or rather–I got excited–in an urban nucleus, there most concretely:

a) a plaza:

b) streets that cross, as long as, and this is key, we speak of a city with a checkerboard layout. For, as I've already said, as the opera says: we must cross paths!

Doubtless, my theory incorporated a wide margin for error, but desperation has its logic. I asked myself what the oldest building was I knew of. And I answered that it was the old belltower. Sure, it's gothic but, I reasoned, if a Roman road went there, could it be far? And who might know? Who is that wise? Him, I said to myself, him! The Autistic Philosopher! It had been some time since I'd paid any mind to Kanguno, but just then, as if in agreement, he wagged his tail. He had tracked my reasoning and approved.

We set off at our optimal pace. I'm going to bring her back –I thought– I'm going to bring you back, a fine end to our story we shall make.

Yet upon reaching the Kibbutz, an uproar startled us: a demonstration being suppressed with mustard. Well, wicked as it may be, I'll admit: I had come to despise the masses. An agglomeration, even if it flew the flag of a just cause, disgusted me. From where arose such strong agreement? From a lived experience, no: there is in the world no theater so grand nor valley so narrow that would allow so many to undergo the same thing. Direct witnesses are not so numerous. I have never, for example, loved, hated, or struggled with the words of another. Had they?

Still, what was truly terrifying: what if you were in the crowd? Surely not, but if somehow you were in the middle of the uproar, would I recognize you? Only if I were still able to bring your features to mind. For example, you have a medium complexion, brown hair, a strong chin...In short, as I began to list off your characteristics, it surprised me how many of those faces also allowed this description and how, packed shoulder-to-shoulder, they, hauntingly or in some other way, defined you. Not you, of course, but the way to describe you. And yet they did define you. Through words? Didn't I just say I don't believe in words? What was all that about, and how to get out of its labyrinth?

CHAPTER 22. FLASHBACK

We waited for the demonstration to disperse. It was on the other side of the Kibbutz, a sort of slum with the afterglow of the sun. And a straight shot from there, a church with a steeple, cylindrical, and tall indeed but not more so than the bunks: the belltower. Before its gate, which had been left open, we saw an ambulance waiting...No! A presentiment. A blackness.

–Stop, ahoy vehicle! Please, tell me who you're here for?

–For no one, a good-for-nothing. Who might you be? Oh look, it's the four-eyes!

–I demand an answer: Who are you here for?

–For no one, I already told you, for an impotent, a suicide...

And the ambulance pulled away, no urgency, no lights, no siren...I had to satisfy my curiosity, I had to know. And so we climbed. We climbed the ladder, the ladder, the ladder. I saw the typewriter, the banquet table whose far end was interred in the clouds. Nothing more. Blindfolded mirrors. Everything was empty and a kind of clinical smell prevailed that disquieted Kanguno.

The story of that man compelled me. Yes, I had to tell his story, take it to the Kibbutz news desk. But how to begin. Would I employ the storytelling techniques I'd acquired? The poetics of Ancila? I would depict not the Philosopher's decline, only his turbulent...freedom. We returned to our bunk. Kanguno made a donut at the foot of the bed and exhaled as though deflating. With some skill I tossed a petticoat over him and tried to concentrate, to imagine the unfortunate man's final moments. It should be a kind of backwards flash, perhaps a flash fiction: the suicide, edicius eht? The main thing was to invert the chronological order, upstream it, until the triumph of life over death was achieved.

In the first scene, an ambulance was bumbling up the ladder. Two nurses came out and grabbed the deceased, set him inside, and left. Then a time lapse during which the Philosopher lay prone. Finally, after the agony, he took a whole bottle of pills, sat, stood up. He seemed uneasy. He would sit at the table and get to typing. That's all. Naturally, he was a failure all over again... In fact, he managed to put icing on his autistic cake: ~No, this is no tragedy, he told me, this is neither tragedy nor comedy. Though its silliness cracks me up. That, that's it: a tragedhehehe, an eleghehehe! –I laughed all through my skeleton.

CHAPTER 23. URSUS ARCTOS HORRIBILIS

And if we meet? What then? Because at the end of time, how many, how many stories will we have consumed? And if we advance one into an encounter with the other and it results in our crossing paths? And if we cross paths, will each, back-to-back, continue to stare into the void, as after thirty, as after sixty steps? I will shout: Draw! And you will understand. We'll make up the rest. And we'll shoot each other. Who knows, one fiction may cure another fiction. And we'll slither along. And we'll embrace on the ground. Like Tristan and Isolde. Something will be embowered, time, or rather, it will be dis-embowered. Surely.

So I believed. I was dreaming until a rocket exploded in the bunks. At the height of forty-one. Utter terror. And I leapt from bed with a start. To the little ladder. There was scarcely time to do anything. Except to yield, to surrender the Kibbutz.

I climbed down to thirty-nine. It was the last time I spoke with him:

> –You here? What do you want? Look, go, climb down to your bed and leave me in peace. – Barefooted, Shanks put his feet upon an atlas: –Look, my footprint, looks just like Eurasia. If I set my heel in Spain, my big toe can reach all the way to Manchuria, and if I really try, uguggh, it crosses the Bering Strait. Here comes Greenwich with its pole! Hey friend! I got you, all China, all the USSR, I plant my foot on all the USSR!
> –Ursus arctos horribilis...Armitage, look, I haven't gone,

here I am, nor do I have the strength to go anywhere let alone a reason to gather my strength. I ask only, for you and for me: you still have time, you can still surrender.

–That's it, right on, let's surrender! Will you surrender first? Come here, that's an order! Come closer to my bear foot! Why come to see me? Don't you know how to do anything yourself? Come, sublime us, work the miracle, make us all die for beauty. Isn't that it? Beauty! How dost thou speak of beauty with your coat all full of holes? Beauty, yes, uguggh...

Suddenly, he brought a hand to his chest as if in his guts something had ripped apart. The page of the atlas under his foot tore. Nevertheless, he recovered himself, flung his hand over the side of the bunk. Signed below:

CHAPTER 24. A BOOK IN WHICH YOU SAVE ONLY YOURSELF

–Exposito, gaze upon Beauty! – Indeed, the Kibbutz never looked like this before. Hunger swelled. The malnourished wandered among other malnourished so that you could hardly tell one from the other. Some streets had thinned out into others and were dubbed ghettos.

Though similarly dazed and worn down, I persisted in my madness, in truth with no conviction, as one who counts sheep without falling asleep. So much sorrow and so much beauty was in the world; and vice versa, in the world was so much beauty and so much sorrow. In other words –keeping score in my head– death exists, horror exists, and yet dazzling passion exists. And if it's a fact that fate hinders enjoyment, I'd swear that the opposite is equally true, that in a certain states of consciousness beauty eclipses all else: time, evil.

Like a bloodhound Shanks seemed to sniff out my associations:

–Do it then, climb, climb the column! Upside down firefighter, all for today! –he wide-smiled –Clark comes by sea in a rage, or in more than one, for he has allied with the dollar-tinted extraterrestrial. But you're scared, yes? The rockets frighten you? That's why you've stuck with Papa Grizzly...

–Clark will arrive before the cock's crow.

–So I'll order all cocks killed! And I'll order the stomping of all crickets!

–Why not surrender? Was the Sherpa not enough for you? You think I've forgiven that?

–Exposito, the kid never existed. Your imaginary friend. Childhood is the Olympus of your autism. The orgasm of your impotence has covered peaks in elemental snows. For far too long we've let you run away with yourself. But you lost all good sense and started screwing around, going from palace to brothel, brothel to palace...Oolala! Are you going to lay hands on me? Well, that's okay, we're going to cut a deal: you answer my question and I'll be your punching bag. Just tell me this: do you truly feel compassion? –that caught me off guard: –You'll say yes, but allow me to complicate things: aside from your obsession, aside from your childhood and aside from that tart wandering through your rustiness, do you feel anything? Answer: Do you actually feel it? Because if you did, you would take to the streets. But "they" mean nothing to you, they mean even less to you than they do to me. Using their lives, I write my nihilistic poem. But you? You don't love. And that love you claim was in fact only the parapet of your vertigo. You know it's true. And despite that you're writing a book in which you save only yourself! Don't forget, you're a worm. So now tell me, you still feel like reining me in?

There he was, happy as a cat's claw. He had made his arrogance shine and his eyes narrowed on mine. Then he finished:

–Incidentally, you don't remember your father either. You're the only orphan who can't. You think he'd be proud? And now leave me to eat in peace.

He pressed a button. A tray popped out from a squeaking sheave; it was his favorite dish: sour cherries canned with the saliva of little girls. As Shanks set about spooning it, I obeyed. I climbed down the ladder, all the ladder. Empty streets. Sand. Women. Men. Dark winters pregnant with absurd, miniscule days: faint sun, weak heat. Once more the sky covered itself with Thy Neighbor Clouds.

CHAPTER 25. CONCERTO FOR CYLINDER

And it snowed. It was the deep snowfall of the Kibbutz and, at the same time, the end. How quiet it all was, quiet cold: the wall, the wheat carousel, the distances holding vigil over Thy Birth Land, the train track, the river that was actually a bed of flowing blonde hair. All was silent. Well, not exactly.

For suddenly cutting the air came what first I believed to be a whaling vessel's horn. It seems to emanate from the old bell-tower. Yes, when the wind enlatches itself within the tower, it produces a whistle, but never multiple different notes let alone a chord. I imagine a giant blowing through it. It sounded, it sounded several times.

Just then a boy in a gunnysack with hair tousled like a cockfight crows:

–Hurray! We are saved, haha!

–Saved how? –they ask.

–It's Kimberly Clark. He's here. With their backs, the rebels cover the windows of the old belltower, so the curly wind whistles instructions to...the Hero. Bearing rockets and firecrackers and loaded up with basilisks, he's coming to our rescue, hahaha.

Far from putting me at ease, my disquiet increased. Kimberly Clark would not be kind. Perhaps I could stow myself in So-babyette's horse-drawn carriage, but for how long? A day? Two? I thought back to Inauguration Day. I recalled the castle of vertical fires. For now the fiesta would be horizontal; we were at war. I wondered if the Moorish geckos would travel through the soil. And would the wolves scale walls? What danger! The world had been turned backward, though no, that wasn't quite right, it was a world rotated ninety degrees Swiss: only Death was not dead, while all else ended in a draw. But what right did I have to complain? Maybe if I had risked my life to come at him guns blazing, forcing him to surrender, saving as many as I could?

Shanks was not going to surrender. To the contrary, he had circled around him the children of the Kibbutz, those called the Worm Youth. He gifted them kites because kites are rockets in larval state. He was speaking to them. He wanted to calm them down. Calm down.

> –How the snow fell in those genetic days, upon the mountains of the Thy Birth Forest. Such snows! Much deeper than these. We made a snowman so massive that it took more than seven men to hug its whole body.
>
> –And you enjoyed this? -the children asked.
>
> –Huh? Did I enjoy it? –He asked perplexed: –Is that what you're asking?
>
> –Yes, that's what we saiiiiiid...Did you enjoy them wrapping their arms around the snowman?

But Shanks didn't know how to respond. Already his language and all his negative theology had been reduced to mere horse racing. It would never have occurred to him to make up a story. For example, that snowmen and scarecrows are of the same species and that only the melting of the ice age separated their evolutionary process.

Then again: was I capable of speaking up? My soul was a hippodrome of timorous horses. I had found it thanks to him. So, I turned to look at him. And I was shaken. He had seated himself on the curb and once more was pressing his hand to his breast. He narrowed his eyes. The children took no notice. He fell over. Then yes, they all cried out then, all of them a single cry. I felt my blood thundering in my temples. What to do. Once again, I know not how, same as on the day with the Sherpa, I did not stand down. I stuffed Kanguno inside my fur coat and stealthily climbed down from bunk to bunk. Suddenly, the heeltaps of some soldiers could be heard. But not the Worm Brigade. No more of them. Some impeccably uniformed orphans thronging Shanks. You must. Yes. Flee.

I hid my head inside the coat and, glancing out through the holes left by the cut sleeves, took off running. Whether they saw me or not, I can't say. I squawked, spaquawked, vasquawked. And I don't know at what point they stopped pursuing me, if they had pursued me at all; but there he was, in the middle of the razed Kibbutz. And as night fell and I drew near Sobabyette's horse-drawn carriage, I repeated to myself a verse I'd once written:

The night grows before the nightingale.
And it grew, full of underdogs, twisted trees for the undecideds hanging.

At last, I came to the horse-drawn carriage. Sobabyette was very thin, gristly, as though bloodless; now his clothes were more covered than ever with embroidery, denser and more baroque.

I throw my arms around the Nutcracker's leg. Kanguno takes cover in a corner. I draw back the curtain of the horse-drawn carriage and peer through the broken window. I'm hungry, cold, afraid. Though hunger wins out. And so I look to the sky, clouds breaking apart; the new moon a wormhole of cheese. I pull the curtain closed.

CHAPTER 26. A CROSS OF LEAD FALLS INTO A LAKE

There came a knock at the carriage door.

> –Ah, from Century XVII, haha. Anyone there? Where did you manage to get this antique? –We looked at each other. The Nutcracker resumed his chattering and I had to stick a sock in his mouth. –Anyone there –the voice repeats. Don't you want to come out here? Nice, here we go...provisions! The war is over, haha. Happy day, comrades! –And through the carriage window he tosses four envelopes and a small herald: "Comrades?" we wonder; Celebrate what? And what was that giggling about.

When the footsteps depart, I take a peek and see that same boy with the hair like a cock fight from the day before.

Kanguno threw himself on the envelopes. It was bread, half a slice in each envelope. Sobabyette began turning purple with each nibble of that bread, as tough as it was well wrapped. I thought back on Shanks, glanced at the communiqué. He was quite ill. They'd had him arrested. Inside the carriage the tension was unbearable. We peered out through knots in the wood. After a moment I stood:

> –Stay with Kanguno, Sobabyette, I'm off to run an errand.
> –You're going now? Where to?

Total ruination all around. The planes of Clark's ally, the dollar-colored alien, soared over the Kibbutz dumping aid kits, the confetti of his color. Of course, there was nowhere to redeem the aid, but the extraterrestrial knew well what he sowed.

Though they had no wish to disclose it, the wounded were many. Just then, I tripped over a tube on account of a saline drip hanging on a pole being stuck in the snow and sending canulae in all directions. As was the case with bread, the saline shortage was severe, but who could keep from marveling at how the tubes scaled stairs, entered doors, rounded corners, and wound themselves into trees. The pole looked like the good shepherd's staff with canulae in place of ribbons. The situation: no saline to be had, but propaganda, influence, oh yes.

I made my way to the Sherpa's tomb, my Pantheon to Childhood. No longer was a flag raised, not of the Shooting Stars nor the Worms. Like harlots on the arms of lords, nights and days had passed by that tomb. That tomb? There was, in fact, no tomb. Just a handful of nettles buried in frost. I kneeled: Had I really dreamed it all? And what all was it? Where did it begin and where did it end?

> ~No, Lord, when I die, my intelligence shall not illuminate a school of fish. May your face forgive me. –For in light of that whole earthquake, I pitied a God orphaned like us, fearful in his act of surrender, incapable of reunion, a God who in vain begat a prince so that his reign might finally end. The tragedy of Creation had to conclude. Yet to mirrors we were condemned, all because instead of loving each other we constructed a temple: ~Lord lost and nailed to the cross like a frog on a reed or an addition sign; oh cross of lead sinking in one lake and another lake, three

lakes, lake upon lake. Will other crosses of lead keep falling into the lake? Yes, variation exists, chaos exists, but if there is salvation, it will come as closure. With earthquakes God rocks the Tomb of the Orphans. Even for heroes the time has come to head home: to corrupt love through repeating it, an amorous tongue; to convert presence into an adoration. The plastic flower in the spring breeze. Yes, this was where Shanks went astray, the very place I'd gone astray. I knew it now: to further expand the exception and to yearn for it, to project it into an order or into a regime. Awaiting it. Denying it. Not leaving it to chance. This was why all that happened had happened, the war -Shanks, Clark, Clark, Shaayaaayaaanks. This was why it was lasting.

When I lift my head, I notice that a specialized breeze is gently lifting the ice crystals. And as it persists and persists, I watch it closer, and to my amazement it begins to write words in the rime:

~Water it…

–What???!!!

~Water it during a full moon.

–Huh? Water what?

~Use…your toys.

–What are you saying? What toys? Who are you? Juan! Juan Boy! Sherpa, is that you?

~……

–Thank you, thank you, Juan Boy!!

But, snapping out of it, I realized: I was surrounded.

–I told you already we had our man, haha.

–Did you think you'd escape, four-eyes, lunatic? –His cackle scrawled an aurora borealis across the sky.

CHAPTER 27. IT ALL COMES TOGETHER

A well, I was led to a well. A well-digger had me squat in a bucket tied to a rope, and he lowered me down, vertiginously, to the bottom of an icicle-lined hole in which not even echoes lodged. Then he raised the bucket and night fell. Each dawn they would throw me down a couple envelopes with bread slices. I knew nothing else. And Sobabyette? Did the guillotine await, that combination window and barber's basin?

Well, the Sherpa's posthumous instructions were still with me:

~Water it on the full moon, use your toys.

Full moon? I looked up. How was I to know if it was waxing or waning? For if you are down a well waiting for the full moon to reach your little circle of sky, you're wishing for a single golf hole with a great many holes. And that wasn't going to happen. I had as my only reference the night before, when I looked upon the sky from the horse-drawn carriage. How handy a lunar calendar would have been!

~Use your toys.

No, no, no sense in that. I searched my right pocket: your girlhood laces, yet I was unwilling to get them dirty; I put them back. I reached a hand into my left pocket: the happened-upon bibelot, Sobabyette's hourglass and, finally, the Sherpa's fingernails.

~ In case one day you can't see the moon.

It was all coming together! It was thus I fashioned a lunar calendar from the fingernail clippings and the buttons of my fur coat. If I didn't die from cold or from their executing me, I still had, according to my shivering calculations, fourteen days of waxing moon left before I "watered it." But water what?

~Where does the sand in the hourglass come from? You think its desert sand, that it's barren? The sand of my Auteuil hourglasses?

I had a special use for each toy except one: the bibelot of snow. Was I to break the bibelot with its stored-up nostalgia and water the hourglass sand with its magnetic juice? I'd do all of this, yes, complying step-by-step with the instructions from the story, its morphology.

I got ready to wait. Over the ensuing fourteen days, nothing major happened. Sometimes the small circle of sky clouded over and it drizzled, which had to mean the temperature was ticking up. Yes, outside, but not at the bottom of the well. Sniffles. Premonitions. Four mornings hearing the chain of a bicycle and a few envelopes with falling bread slices, which I devoured. More sniffles. More premonitions. That was it.

On the seventh day, I grew rather nervous; the well stones appeared to me as faces from the crowd of a suffocating circus: Countenances of the Adoration? Had that nonsense followed me all this way? I pulled out the bibelot one last time to admire it, its snowman; he was perfection. "Tomorrow," I told him. I returned the bibelot, curled up against a wall, and buried my hand in the pocket filled with laces.

CHAPTER 28. THE ASCENSION OF THE TEARS

The day had come, but I waited for its night, for the moon. I did. I freed the hourglass from its wooden frame. Next, I cracked the glass of the bibelot against the well stones and poured the contents of the hourglass onto the sand. All night, I watched over my experiment. Open eyes like owls, owlets. And nothing. Only hours. The cross of lead had sunk in the lake, the lake, the lake. Silence, but no peace, the well. Would the miracle work when the sand dried? It dried, dawn came. Morning passed just the same. Just the same.

But at three in the afternoon, as the thinnest ray of sun crept in, I beheld an ant emerging from the hourglass sand. An ant, yes, as though it had passed the night beneath the desert and was now leaving its hiding place. It scampered up my sleeve, lost itself in my clothes, strode through the well stones, those I'd called the Countenances of the Adoration.

That was it. Was fate toying with me? A tragedhehehe? An eleghehehe? I was terrified. I had complied with every rule of that game, one-by-one, each marvelous object from the marvelous tale and its framework, but no nothing, no function, no action. The ant liberation? TOUGH TASK? TRANSFIGURATION? COMBAT? JOURNEY? RETURN? I was afraid. I was going to die, like all men, thinking of you, as a man. A – the; determinate article – indeterminate article. Abandoned.

The story, my story. I went through puberty inside a fat kid. My father and my childhood died together. But you came along with a spare one. You had shattered a pearl necklace upon the world and the beads had rolled inside empty oysters. This was you, a REPAIR, love. And yet, undoubtedly, Shanks had a point, now I knew it; yes, I loved you, but you were also my guardrail when I ventured out to test the urgent and incomplete essence of the beautiful. Perhaps you were not just another of my trading cards; maybe the entire set, I don't know. But I was the one, I abandoned us. And now I insulted you by calling you Beauty, by equating you with that blended perfume of forms.

All at once, I saw the image crystal-clear: It was those final days, in your room, when I'd turned myself into a heartless, stubborn dilettante, an expert instead of a lover. You turned to me and said: "Don't insult me." And you cried. You cried then and I cry now. I sat upon a rock and wept, wept into my glasses, and from there onto the hourglass. I wept and the warmth of the tears made me drowsy.

The following day, I was in a stupor. Was it the tears? A green stalk had sprouted from the hourglass and was lost, lost in the sky! The folk tale came to my rescue! And I climbed, no clue how I did it, me, the klutz, but I climbed and didn't stop. I left behind the well, a treeless terrain, and felt no urge to stop; I saw the Kibbutz from on high, the train track, the mountain with the suitcase shape, the blonde river gushing through the gorge, Thy Birth Country. I thought I could make out even the little Mountain Hamlet. After climbing the stalk for some time, I grew fearful, for an eagle was circling. Then I pressed on; up and up I went, into the cloud.

CHAPTER 29. *PULL IT OK!*

When I reach the top, I see a serpentine, what could be called a high mountain road. In the distance, a stationary vehicle, and stepping from it, the silhouette either of someone about to slip and split their head or of someone simply slipping off their overcoat, impossible to say. I approach. For some reason, I sensed that silhouette had something to do with God. He advances with long and wayward strides and I pursue thinking that if I do speak with Him, I'll have no margin for error with my questions, as had Perceval. Suddenly, I see the silhouette entering an octagonal church which brings to mind the de-legged spider of the yes and the no. In the portico, a girl selling saint cards – Ancila? –she sits at a table with drawers. The girl sprouts hair at such a clip that she's forced to store it in drawers, but she can't keep up and her hair runneth over.

I enter the church. Its retablo consists of a cleft between two Cyclopean rocks that converge to communicate with The Something and where I lose sight of the silhouette that either slipped and fell or slipped on the half-coat. I keep after it. Just as I'm about to enter the cleft, my heart begins to race. I am aware that beyond this point I must live with emptiness as possibility. Same as you?

The light was other, utterly. This sensation was accentuated by the quite high ceilings of the Nothing. A space lined with mirrors in which angels rehearse. My heart nearly leapt from me, leaped from my chest. Then, I don't know why, I started beating the mirrors with my fists, and they shattered just like eggshells. I set about tearing shards from between the strips of albumen; once they were peeled, a padded wall was revealed, like a holding cell in a mental institute.

Suddenly, chimes behind me. I turn. Yes, the chimes of…a slot machine! And on top of the machine, a glowing sign:

pull it ok!

What's this? Another joke? Whatever it was, I wasted no time in pulling the crank. The three wheels began to spin; they spin like the pleasing rustling of ossicles, destination letters on the marquee of an old train station. They spin until each of them rests at, respectively:

a bell | a cherry | an id photo
of my father

Below the wheels, the buttons chime now with another sound, a noise of colors. I press the one below the bell and the wheel spins and spins until landing on:

an id photo | a cherry | an id phot
of my father   of my father

The buttons chime anew and I press the cherry. The wheel spins and spins and spins until it holds:

an id photo | an id photo | an id photo
of my father   of my father   of my father

Just then, a little tune plays. My father's favorite. Father? And now a door fringed with neon red cable comes into view. The door opens to a room in a hospital, a bed in there against the wall. To my surprise and despite my anxiety, the lenses of my glasses did not blush.

–Dad, I didn't want...I didn't want to bring you here again, no, no I will not sublimate myself...Not for beauty nor for love; I'm going to die, I'm going to die, I inherited it from you.

Then I leaned over his bed, wanting to kiss him, but as I drew near and breathed upon his brow a few of his eyelashes fell off. I blew, and all his lashes flew off like silk from a thistledown. My father spoke to me:

~If you blow on me, I have cancer.

And I wept deeply from both eyes until a wind like the Spirit of Christmas Past returned me to the cloud. I took off running, ran like a man possessed until my foot sank. The cloud spread into spongy skerries and I started hopping from one to the next. During one hop, my glasses flew off. Finally, I stood in some kind of cotton candy. I removed my coat, clenched a corner of it and a flap with each hand, improvising a fur parachute, and I leapt.

CHAPTER 30. THE HANGING FOREST,
THE RIVER GONE GREY

I managed to survive but hit the corner of my eye on a branch, while my ankles had grown so weak that I could scarcely stand up. So I stretched out in the grass. Time must have passed more rapidly up there, because I was lying in overgrown grass of a season that was no longer red, blue, or yellow, but freely summer.

Was it a dream I'd lived up there? A dream? Hahaha! At a wake with concrete footings? Nothing seemed certain anymore. Of course, no trace of the green stalk remained, nor were there clouds of any sort in the sky. Not one shred of evidence, save one, yes: my glasses really had disappeared…

I did not understand, but neither did I expect to understand. I was worn thin. In fact, I fell asleep, and it was only after waking up that I got around to asking myself where I was. My myopia aside, it was not difficult to ascertain: once more, the dangling forest. Yet, my God…they had felled the fir trees! Only nooses dangled lugubriously, the hanging forest! Had all the neighboring trees suffered the same fate? Yet this surprise was not the only one, for when I approached the river, which was a bed of undulating blonde hair, I could see…it was grey! The hair had gone grey! Confronted with these visions, which recalled for me Sobabyette's apocalypse, I wanted, for the first time in my life, to end it all. I fashioned a bundle from my clothes and leaning over the grey-haired river saw myself reflected. That's when I discovered I had a black eye from being struck by the branches.

First, I stuck in one foot, then the other; next, my legs up to the knees. A shudder. I was the most ludicrous of suicides. I exited the river. Ankles sore, I lay for a good long while on my back.

My naked body, my face white with a lilac roundel, and the lilac sky with a full moon that I could see when I squinted. We were coming to resemble each other, yin and yang were we. I should have felt myself crossed by a helical current, but far from it, in no cosmos was I contained. It was just me, a wretched obstacle between the Milky Way and recumbent Earth.

My eyelids shrouded the sky.

CHAPTER 31. «SI TU VIENS, PAR EXAMPLE , À QUATRE HEURES DE L'ÀPRÈS-MIDI, DÈS TROIS HEURES JE COMMENCERAIS D'ÊTRE HEUREUX» (SAINT EXUPÉRY)

The following day, or rather, yesterday, for the story is already over, I awoke to Kanguno's tongue licking my face. And a small, painfully red doll that could be none other than the Nutcracker: I hugged them:

–Friends! How did you find me? Then I was afraid to ask: And Sobabyette? Where is he?

The Nutcracker took out a notebook and began to write:

–We take refuge now in The-Iron-Chain-In-Bloom-*Non-Stop-Show*. My lord is quite ill. Come.

Thus, with some difficulty, I dressed and, with Kanguno supporting me, limped the whole way there, with the little Nutcracker steering our expedition. As we went along, we squinted just to see. Now everything looked worse. If possible. Poverty had been reduced, but where were the bunks, the trees, the lakes? All was smoke, noise, traffic and a wind farm that many sat before, cooling off. Not a star to be seen; the Kibbutz had transformed into a great city and in great cities the sky holds fewer stars, just as abridged books hold fewer words.

We came to the doorway of The-Iron-Chain-In-Bloom. As on the last day of Sobabyette's palace, cranes encircled the area.

We entered. The dragon had lost some teeth:

T- T-H- G- -R-L-S

Limping, I beat a path to where Sobabyette lay. Beyond skinny, gristly, his clothes more covered than ever with embroidery that was rococo now, hermetic.

I passed a long night with him while he caught me up on the latest, his voice growing thin and his language more charged with hyperbaton, more nasally; a long night in which I wrote this entire story in the Nutcracker's notebook; a long night that lasted until dawn when I began the final chapter saying...

CHAPTER 32. BOUND FOR THE CAPE OF LACES

And no longer can I live your life
and no longer can I live mine

Claudio Rodríguez

Sobabyette had died. I drew near to blow out the candle of his hand. Incensed, he had died, my friend, relating to me, until he perished, what had happened.

Kimberly Clark had ordered the church torn down on grounds it was unstable, for thrust and pressure through its ribs and arches were not keeping it erect, but rather controversies around sexual morality. Moreover, he had set fire to his figurines, convinced that saints and martyrs are useless, for they lose faith and devote their time to the tallying of pustules.

On the other hand, the old belltower still stood. International fanfare rang out from it daily, accompanied by expensive fireworks. Quite expensive, yes indeed, so much so, it seemed, that they found it necessary to open the belltower as a tourist attraction. It had not been difficult to do; the stone of the steps was worn smooth in the center and was already like a toboggan.

Indeed, the city had also opened itself to foreign merchandise. I reasoned out that Clark had failed to stop an unstoppable machine: if men have grown accustomed to trading in their dreams for products, it follows that the forms of those products must go around and around, attaining a hypnotic rhythm and transforming so none may escape the delusion. It wasn't strange, really, that hypnosis had attained unprecedented levels of sophistication. Apparently, the very same Clark had ordered the manufacture of a limousine simply because he'd become enchanted with a blurry photo of an ordinary car. Regarding the instituted regime, I believe they called it Tolerance: an anonymous political system founded upon an inanimate unanimity. That was why tolerance was exercised, first and foremost, with respect to anomalies and injustices intrinsic to the system and, it was said, with respect to the production of merchandise.

Before his death Sobabyette had said: the end times had offered us another reason for abandoning the world, our inability to adapt ourselves to great changes, and great ugliness.

Okay, enough is enough. We've made up our minds. We won't bat an eyelid, let the cranes in. Perhaps Kanguno will bark, I don't know. Dawn is breaking. For the last time I approached the corpse of my friend, his fingernails purpled, his body swelled: together in him now are blood and piss, forgetting the great zeal the organism utilized to keep them separate; reconciled now are the divine and the horrible, after so many years listening to the Ave Verum and frequenting a Chinese dragon. Rest, Sobabyette.

It's time for me to end the story. The motors of the cranes are running; lusting, leveling. A disheveled ivy climbs toward the dawn's dim moon. But it is no symbol of consummation. There is no consummation. It was already, it already happened. There is only a lake and a cross of lead. For us these must suffice.

I, on the other hand, was wrong for forgetting your presence, for awaiting you in other forms. As I said before, I was a merchant of your possibility, an expert and not a lover; I wanted to merge two diverse tendencies and, even worse, I ignored your arrival, that the miracle was you. Yet it's also true that for a few hours Armitage Shanks and Kimberly Clark were revolutionaries. My project was just as monstruous. I also utilized tools and ladders, I, too, desired an experiment, to die for beauty. What made me different from them, I who waited for the very same morning, I who held you and betrayed you.

And my friends? They are at peace. Even the Nutcracker, though he was now on his own, cut free. Kanguno sleeps. Maybe God does speak to us and his voice is like those ultrasonic whistles only dogs can hear. Maybe God whistles to animals and so they have no fear. Or not too much.

Even I am no longer fearful. Let this be my pharaoh's tomb, one for an obsessed fool. Set fire to this decrepit dragon. So long, Adoration.

This I have written; these words will be my last.

Now I lay me down and bury my hand in my pocket. Let us go, my right hand, set a course for the Cape of Laces.

THE END

.

CHAPTER 33. POEM?

All night they hear the many birds.
In the morning the sky astounded
quickly composed a cloud to have
a head and to turn it: a cloth Chinese dragon
threaded sky and threaded the calendar
backwards; spring, winter,
the nineteenth of December,
one year and another.
The larks also returned
a far away from supplicating
balconies and now accustomed
to clattering heels on the Boeings' ground,
serpents set free from spells
and even the abyssal fish leaping from
the water. To behold it.

Not for the rising sea levels
nor for the diminution of the polar ice
would they have hastened
the eternal return. Not one bit.
It just was. It took place.
On the day they fell in love the Chinese dragon
from The-Iron-Chain-in-Bloom touched down,
opening his mouth, rolling out the carpet
of his tongue so that Exposito and his dog
might emerge with greater luxury than
did Jonah from the cetacean,

while on his fangs
it read: "H-E-R-E-Y-O-U-A-R-E."

For there she was and, doing up her hair
–colors to your posts!–, she tied a lace
across which tumbled sleepy squirrels.
This was no semblance; it was the very day
of the red poppy on her thigh,
when they met and he had a wormhole
in his sole that whistled as he walked.
It sounded then. Just the same.
Only now a dog wagged his tail,
as if in agreement.

They ran, they hugged each other,
they spoke the words –the two Greek Is
and the two Latin Is– silly ones
in a language of two, those words that shiver
if ever the duo are separated,
for in this world they shall have
no other speakers.
No one comes anymore, a desert
of hourglass sand, of time,
indeed, of the other,
for their moment had occurred.
Not even a laurel, no grapevine,
nor a mosaic declaring:
Cave Cangunem, even the fork
and the spoon loved each other here.

A guard asked: But these glasses…?
I swear I saw them fall from the sky.

–Don't they belong to the weirdo,
the four-eyes? Wasn't he taken to a well?
–No one knows.
–Then toss them into the river, save us some trouble.

And the glasses saw themselves falling
down a waterfall,
surrounded by toucans and water dust,
falling until the end of time
or until another ice age
drops them into the shovel of
the universe's snowplow.
The hand on the knocker bid goodbye.
Things had returned
to live within their colors
though they were now free:
and there you could see the snow shedding
its white like a kid taking off his pajamas,
and the sky its blue
and the wheat its yellow.

Until side-by-side, without
casting a reflection, they bathed.

AMEN